D1797935

Dealing With
the
Spirit of Disappointment

DS VOLUME 21

Bishop Climate Irungu

Copyright © 2016 by Bishop Climate Ministries

All rights reserved. No part of this publication may be reproduced, distributed or transmitted in any form or by any means, including photocopying, recording, or other electronic or mechanical methods, without the prior written permission of the publisher, except in the case of brief quotations embodied in critical reviews and certain other noncommercial uses permitted by copyright law. For permission requests, write to the publisher, addressed "Attention: Permissions Coordinator," at the address below.

Bishop Climate Ministries
PO Box 67884
London, England SE5 9JJ
www.bishopclimate.org
Email: prayer@bishopclimate.org
Tel: +44 7984 115900 (UK)
Tel: +44 207 738 3668 (UK)
Tel: +732 444 8943 (USA)

Contents

The Book of Job

Caravans turn aside from their routes; they go off into the wasteland and perish. The caravans of Tema look for water, the traveling merchants of Sheba look in hope.

They are distressed, because they had been confident; they arrive there, only to be disappointed.

Now you too have proved to be of no help; you see something dreadful and are afraid. Have I ever said, 'Give something on my behalf, pay a ransom for me from your wealth, deliver me from the hand of the enemy, rescue me from the clutches of the ruthless'? (Job 6:18-23 NIV)

PART ONE

What is the Spirit of Disappointment?

In January of 2009, God spoke to me that for the entire year I must only read the book of Job. I had read through the entire Bible a couple of times before but I never really paid attention to the book of Job.

Because of who Job was and the knowledge that he had; the devil himself had a respect for him. He was a wise man; God showed him how to do commerce and how to flourish in times of Egypt. Even Pharaoh would consult with him.

Everything that Job speaks about is valid and applicable for us today. The time that Job lived in was a time where information was rampant, just like how it is today.

When the Lord began showing me about the book of Job, I realized that it has a wealth of information that we can use for our own advantage.

There is no other account in the Bible quite like Job, a man who suffered incredible hardship, losing all of his children, all of his business, all of his property. A respected man, one of incredible stature becoming like a lowly beggar whom others would gawk at. A man who was regularly called upon for wise counsel was suddenly being criticized by his closest friends. And if anyone was familiar with the spirit of disappointment, it was this man.

But Job knew something that others didn't. He had an understanding about the spiritual realm, and it is what gave him confidence. The knowledge that Job had about the spiritual world was the key to his break-through. When everyone else turned against him, he knew what was going on and he refused to turn against himself. And that is why you need this understanding, so that you too can make it over to the other side.

A spirit of disappointment is a demon assigned from hell to be able to push you off course or frustrate you to the point of quitting. It usually works alongside other spirits to accomplish its purpose. It can delay your breakthrough, cause last minute rejections, and hinder others who have been assigned to help you.

Caravans turn aside from their routes; they go off into the wasteland and perish. The caravans of Tema look for water, the traveling merchants of Sheba look in hope.

They are distressed, because they had been confident; they arrive there, only to be disappointed. (Job 6:18-20)

In this chapter, Job is talking about a specific route that the caravans would take. Normally caravans would use a specific route every time. Just like today with planes, trains, etc. they use specific routes that have already been laid out. But what happens when they go off route? They get disappointed; they perish.

Sometimes you see planes perish because they go off route. The plane is equipped with enough fuel based on its scheduled route, but if it takes another route, it doesn't have enough resources to last the trip. Even up to today those situations still cause disappointment, so many families whose lives are on hold because they were never able to find out what happened.

What is it that is always causing you to miss your destination? What is that spirit that is always causing delay here and there? Sometimes you do something that you have done many times before and you are confident of the outcome, but now its just disappointment everywhere. At the last minute everything changes, everything starts to work against you. Today I want to talk to you about the spirit of disappointment, for it is not your portion.

PART TWO

4 Ways the Spirit of Disappointment Operates

1. THROUGH DEMONIC DIVERSION

Caravans turn aside from their routes; they go off into the wasteland and perish. The caravans of Tema look for water, the traveling merchants of Sheba look in hope. (Job 6:18-19)

The scripture says they left their route to go and look for water. They weren't just wandering around looking for water. No, they were confident, they knew where they were headed to; it was a specific place where they would find water.

These caravans were in the desert. If you have never been to the desert before, everything is sand. The only way to make it through successfully is to know the routes and to stick to them. (In fact, since time of old, travellers would read and understand the signs of the stars in order to successfully navigate through the desert). In the desert, water is scarce, but there are particular routes that can lead you to water. And the water is always there no matter the time of year.

So the caravans were taking a specific route that they knew, they had taken it many times before, and that's why they had hope.

But verse 20 says:

They are distressed, because they had been confident; they arrive there, only to be disappointed.

What happened? When they got to the place where the water should be, there was nothing to find. They couldn't just turn back and go another route; there was no time left. They had already used all their efforts, all their resources, taking this other route. When they discovered there was no water, it was too late. And so they perished there in the wasteland, forgotten and all alone.

I see that this is what has been happening to you. You had hope that something was going to happen; something inspired you, something caused hope to rise up in you. You knew that that it was your season, that it was your time, but as soon as you got there you were disappointed.

I see something is always coming to try and distract your focus, to pull you in another direction, so you end up leaving your original plan and focusing on something else, but you just keep getting disappointed. You end up perishing, and you lose what you original-ly had. Satan has been manipulating you, trying to di-vert you to go off course, so he can be able to strangle you slowly and kill your love life, kill your destiny, and kill what God has for you. But every evil forces assigned to assassinate your destiny through disappointment must be exposed before it's too late. That spirit of disappointment, today it must die by fire! Every false hope must die by fire!

2. THROUGH LAST-MINUTE DELAYS & REJECTIONS

They are distressed, because they had been confident; they arrive there, only to be disappointed. (Job 6:20)

Do you know what a mirage is? Basically it is when you see something that's not really there. It happens in the desert or places where there is extreme heat. But it looks so real until you get right up to it and then you realize it never existed.

I see in the realm of the spirit there is a demon that has been summoned to keep postponing your goalpost. So every time you think you have made it, you find that you are even farther away.

How many times have you been in that situation where you know this is the day, you were confident that you were going to get that breakthrough, maybe it was a job, or a breakthrough of some sort, and then suddenly at the last moment you got disappointed. You had confidence that everything would work out; but at the last moment everything changed, everything turned against you, and you found yourself cornered. Today we reject that spirit of disappointment in Jesus name.

I see there is a demon of disappointment that has been summoned from hell to make sure you never get what you want. But I declare Jesus finished well and you are going to finish well too. Today we are going to deal with every demon of disappointment, every spirit that waits till the last moment, until all your hopes are up, and then brings you crashing down, today it must leave. The days of disappointment and postponement are over. Your money must come now; your favor must come now; your job must come now;

your marriage must take place now; your status must come through now!

3. THROUGH ATTACKING THOSE AROUND YOU

Now you too have proved to be of no help; you see something dreadful and are afraid. (Job 6:21)

I told you the spirit of disappointment works alongside other spirits. They work together to attack anyone that wants to help you; they will cause similar issues to happen in their life.

Have you ever seen in the movies where a bad guy is trying to catch someone and they will go and visit a friend or family member of the person and threaten them if they try to help? And out of fear the person will flee and never speak to the person again. This is the same thing that happens spiritually. When there is a spirit of disappointment in your life, it targets those around you, those who have an assignment to help you, those who are supposed to be connected to you.

But this demon begins working on them, hindering them, affecting their lives. That's why you find somebody has promised to help you but at the last moment they pull off without any explanation.

It's not because they wanted to betray you but because the war that they began to experience since they started helping you has scared them. They have never seen anything like it before so slowly by slowly they back off.

Even Jobs friends were of no help to him.

Now you too have proved to be of no help; you see something dreadful and are afraid. (Job 6:21)

What was that something? It was a spirit. They began experiencing the same thing. Disappointments started coming and they realized something was not right.

I see there are some people that wanted to help you but suddenly they were attacked in the dream. Demons showed up using your face as a mask, and strange things began to happen. Since that day they changed the story. They woke up wondering about the dream and began to back off. This is why you keep getting abandoned. Yes someone is now mistaking you as an enemy; someone very close has been deceived through dreams and has turned against you. Someone capable to help you has been falsely warned through this spirit; someone who was assigned to lift you up from that pity has been confused. You must pray and pray now; pray quickly! You must strengthen them through prayers so they can reach you on time.

The same thing happens in relationships. One man kept dreaming at night that a man was coming to him and asking him where his white shirt was and telling him he should ask his wife. He couldn't find the shirt and finally asked the wife. She told him she didn't know where it was either. So he thought she must have been cheating on him and he left her. But that was an evil spirit sent from hell to cause disappointment in their marriage.

Other times a woman can be dating or engaged to a man and suddenly the man starts having strange dreams about her. He thinks there is something wrong so he leaves and never speaks to her again. I have seen many people's lives lost and destroyed by this spirit. It takes an anointing to know how to deal with it. I pray for you now that through these prayers you will no longer fall victim to this spirit.

I see this type of circle keeps going on in your life. Every time somebody is about to favor you they experience a nasty attack and pull away because they don't understand. Somebody is holding the key to your destiny and the devil has been working on them. They were capable of blessing you but suddenly they saw this evil spirit and since then they have been afraid to help you. Now you have just been abandoned, left all alone, because anyone that tries to pick up your case begins to experience trouble.

You see it's the enemy giving them a warning, to stay in their own lane, but they don't realize it's because you are a destiny carrier. They don't realize the devil is so scared of you, he knows you are a generational curse breaker and that spirit doesn't want you to come out of that curse. But everything is about to change in Jesus name.

That rejection, that delay, that disappointment that you have been going through is not normal. No, it is all demonic. Why do you think you have been losing things here and there, all those disappointments, nobody likes you anymore, nobody wants to help you, you feel so abandoned? It's because they are seeing things they have never seen before. Hell has declared war against you! But fear not, you are not alone.

Greater is He that is in us then He that is in the world. (1 John 4:4)

I see you standing up like Job. He refused to quit on himself. He refused to point a finger at himself when everybody else did. Even his own wife told him to curse God and die. But he knew that even if everyone else quit on him, he would not quit on himself. He remained confident that God would come for him.

Have I ever said, 'Give something on my behalf, pay a ransom for me from your wealth, deliver me from the hand of the enemy, rescue me from the clutches of the ruthless'? (Job 6:22)

You have never asked for others' sympathy; no you have never tried getting by on the backs of others. Still the devil has made you like something to mock at, somehow every blame and fault is being put on you.

But today you are going to be delivered from the clutches of the ruthless, that ruthless spirit that has been causing frustration, rejection, fear and torment in your life, die by fire!

Right now I know what is happening in your life; everyone has been condemning you, blaming you for what's going on, nobody wants anything to do with you because from the day they started to help you all hell broke loose in their lives. But realize that the devil is so terrified about your destiny; he is so terrified about your breakthrough. But you are not a quitter.

You have caused men to ride over our heads; we went through fire and through water: but you brought us out into a wealthy place. (Ps 66:12)

I see this scripture becoming your anthem. Yes no disappointment is going to keep you down. Heaven is about to open for you; favor is about to come. Even in the desert you will make it, you are not going to perish.

4. THROUGH A LYING SPIRIT

After this spirit has had a chance to work on you through demonic diversion, last minute delays, and attacking those around you, it begins to work in a more personal way, which can become very damaging in the long run. After you have been disappointed, this spirit works with another spirit called a lying spirit. It will come and speak lies to you telling you to never get your hopes up, reminding you of all the times you have been disappointed in the past, and how this time it's going to be the same. But if you are not careful you can become a self-fulfilling prophecy. Job said, "What I feared the most came upon me". (Job 3:25)

I see the spirit of disappointment has been cast over your mind to the point that you have become so used to disappointment that you just expect it all the time.

I see sometimes people try to do good things for you but you just expect that disappointment to come and you end up fulfilling what you think will happen. You forfeit the good that God and others are trying to do for you. But right now I curse that lying spirit, every form of disappointment that wants to keep you in oppression, that wants to keep you from being happy, that wants to keep you from experiencing the good life that God has for you, I cast it out in Jesus name.

Yes I know that you have been disappointed in the past, but that is in the past. Now that we are going to pray, I want you to start expecting the best. Yes expect the very best, expect people to favor you, expect good things to happen, expect every blessing coming your way.

Deal With the Spirit of Disappointment

I feel so strong that there are some challenges you are going through that were also experienced in your father's house. But they backed off and as a result they lived an ordinary life of oppression and lack. But today that curse must be broken. You must cross that river. As we begin to pray, I declare that what brought your father down, what brought your mother down, will not bring you down in Jesus name. After these prayers, I see the peace of God all around your life.

(As you begin to pray, you may experience coughing and/or vomiting. It is that spirit inside of you that is always telling you that you will be disappointed, it is going to come out in Jesus name).

Before you pray, remember to put on the full armor of God according to Ephesians 6:10-18, touching each part of your body as you say it.

Repeat with me: "I put on the full armor of God. The helmet of salvation upon my head, the breastplate of righteousness in its place, the belt of truth around my waist, my feet shod with the readiness of the gospel of peace, taking the shield of faith in my left hand and the sword of the spirit in my right".

In the Name of Jesus:

1. Right now I take authority over every spirit of disappointment that I have inherited from my fathers house, from my mothers house, I bind you, I rebuke you, die by fire!

2. In the name of Jesus, I declare every spirit of disappointment that has been used to hinder and stop my family members, I bind you, I rebuke you, I defeat you, and I command you to die by fire!

3. I take authority over every demon of disappointment that has been assigned over my life, over my destiny, I bind you, I rebuke you, and I uproot you out of my life in Jesus name.

4. Every demon of disappointment assigned over my life as a result of jealousy, I bind you, I rebuke you, I dismantle you, and I command you to die by fire!

5. Right now I take authority over every spirit of disappointment in my body, in my mind, in my finances, in my marriage, in my family, in my career, in my business, I rebuke you, I bind you, I cast you out! Come out!

6. Every spirit of disappointment that has been assigned over my life to cause last minute delays over my documents, my finances, my marriage, today I command it to die by fire!

7. Every spirit of disappointment, every demon of disappointment that has been playing with my life, I bind it in Jesus name.

8. Every spirit of disappointment that has been causing demonic diversions, I bind it. Every road to disappointment I command it to die by fire!

9. Every sprit of disappointment where my marriage is concerned, die by fire!

10. Every demon of disappointment over my finances I rebuke you in Jesus name!

11. Every demon of disappointment where my career is concerned, where any legal situation is concerned, I command it to die by fire!

12. Every family disappointment, every disappointment over my children and the fruit of my womb, I bind you, I rebuke you, I command you to die by fire!

13. Every demon of disappointment that has been summoned from hell to frustrate my marriage, I command it to die by fire!

14. Every demon that has been attacking those around me, hindering them from helping me, I command it to die by fire!

15. Every evil spirit that has been targeting those who are assigned to help me, making them afraid, causing them to abandon me, I command you to die by fire!

16. Every spirit of witchcraft that has been activated to cause trouble, to cause people not to help me, to cause people to abandon me, I command it to die by fire!

17. I take authority over all those who have been assigned to help me; wherever they are I command them to be released in Jesus name! I command their finances to be released! I command their health to be released! I command their destiny to be released!

18. Every spirit of disappointment that has been summoned to frustrate me until I give up, I command it to die by fire!

19. Every spirit of disappointment that has been assigned over my mind to always expect disappointment in my life, I cast it out in Jesus name!

20. From today I declare and I decree that everyday in every way my life is becoming better and better!

21. From today I declare and I decree that everyday in every way my destiny is becoming better and better!

22. From today I declare and I decree that everyday in every way my future is becoming better and better!

What Can I Expect?

So now that you have your prayer points you need to understand that deliverance is not a onetime event but a process and you need to be consistent if you are going to destroy the enemies in your life. Let's look at a few things you can expect while going through your deliverance.

Firstly, expect to be set free and for peace to return back into your life. The Bible says that those who wait for the Lord shall not be ashamed. Also, start expecting God to give you a testimony, just like everyone else who has gone through our deliverance program.

There are some key steps you can follow to ensure you are doing everything properly in order to obtain your desired goals. (These are in addition to your daily prayer points listed in this book)

1. <u>Locate the area of your need</u>

According to what your situation may be, you need to identify the particular area or areas, which are most dire.

2. <u>Find out what the Word of God says regarding that area</u>

Select the appropriate scriptures promising you what you desire and meditate upon them. Write them on your walls where you can see them. Even if it means writing it on yourself so you won't forget to recite them during the day. Do whatever it takes but make sure you are replaying them in your mind daily.

3. <u>Go through a special prayer in one of the following ways while expecting your deliverance</u>

· 3 day Night Vigil at the Sanctuary (i.e. praying and confessing the Word from 10 pm to 5 am for 3 nights in a row)

· 3 Day Fast (i.e. praying, fasting, and confessing the Word daily from 6 am to 6 pm for 3 days. Alternatively you can fast straight through the 3 days only breaking for communion)

· 3-Day Fast Prayer Vigil at the Sanctuary (i.e. praying, fasting, and confessing the Word daily from 10 am to 6 pm for 3 days. Again you can fast continually for 3 days apart from communion)

· 3 + Days Dry Fast (i.e. praying, fasting, and confessing the Word for 3 or more days without taking food or drink). Please note: This should only be done under pastoral recommendation.

4. <u>Pray aggressively while believing that you receive your deliverance</u>

Hebrews 11:6 says *"we must believe that He is and that He is a rewarder of them that diligently seek Him".*

5. <u>Make any adjustments in your life and repent as the Holy Spirit leads</u>

You have to make sure that you are not leaving any open doors for the enemy to regain access in your life.

6. <u>This is the most crucial step. You must sow your seed to seal your deliverance</u>

Most people sow consecutive seeds, giving it the same name according to their expectation from God regarding their deliverance. To truly succeed in spiritual warfare you have to be a sower. The Bible says in Deut 16:16 to "never appear before God empty handed". So as you are expecting to receive something from

God you need to be giving back something to Him as well.

7. Lastly, prepare yourself for your miracle physically and spiritually

Be vigorous in attending service as much as possible in order to receive the ministration of the Word and the laying on of the hands by the man of God. Also, attend your deliverance sessions regularly if you have been assigned to a mentor.

ABOUT THE MINISTRY

Bishop Climate Ministries is the Healing & Deliverance Ministry founded by Bishop Climate under the anointing and direction of the Holy Spirit. God has anointed Bishop Climate with incredible power to set the captives free. Many people who were unable to get deliverance anywhere else find their freedom as they attend special deliverance sessions conducted through this ministry. The vision of Bishop Climate Ministries is to reach over 1 billion people with the message of deliverance and prosperity, especially in understanding the things of the spirit. Many people are bound because of lack of knowledge and one of the goals of this ministry is to set people free through education.

hild of God I want you to know how much I appreciate you and how special you are to me. That is why God keeps giving me the wisdom to write these books at such a time as this. He sees your heart and wants you to experience the abundant life that Jesus died for. And so do I. Your support for our ministry is crucial and I hope that you will always continue to lift us up in prayer to God.

I want to take this opportunity to encourage you to partner with us at Bishop Climate Ministries. Hundreds have testified of the miracles that have taken place in their life just as a result of sowing into this ministry and I want you to be able to experience that 100 fold return Jesus spoke about regarding sowing seed into good ground. The Bible says in Proverbs 11:24 *"One person gives freely, yet gains even more; another withholds unduly, but comes to poverty"*. Your prayers and financial support are crucial to take this message of salvation and deliverance around the world. And as you do that you can be sure that God is going to bless you beyond your wildest imaginations. There is a 4-fold anointing that you step under when you become a partner with Bishop Climate Ministries. It is the anointing that God has put over my life and this ministry according to Isaiah 11:2. That is the anointing of Divine Direction, Divine Connections, Divine Provision and Divine Protection.

Please understand how much I value you. Your support for our ministry is so crucial and your prayers are as a pillar to us. Your partnership with this ministry is so important and that's why we are committed to praying for you daily and lifting your needs up before God. When you send in your donation please send me a prayer request as well so I can intercede on your behalf before God. I look forward to seeing you in person at our Healing and Deliverance Centre in London, England or at one of our Healing and Deliverance Miracle Crusades.

Remember this is the Ministry where the captives are set free and souls are refreshed.

Remain blessed,

Bishop Climate Irungu

Victory Over The Spirit Of Humiliation & Oppression
Breaking The Curse Of
Good Beginnings & Bad Endings
Victory Over Demonic Assignments
Overcoming Every Generational Hatred
Overcoming Persistent Enemies
Destroying Every Demonic Blockage
Victory Over Every Troubling Spirit
Destroying Every Spirit of Poverty & Lack
Destroying Every Demonic Covenant Over Your Life
Victory Over Every Appointment With Death
Binding the Strongman
Uprooting Every Demonic Prophecy
Victory Over Every Evil Wish
Breaking Every Demonic Spell
Overturning Every Demonic Judgment
Victory Over Every Frustrating Spirit
Destroying Every Demonic Altar
Uprooting Every Territorial Sorcerers

Victory Over Demonic Storms (Marine Spirit)
Dealing With the Spirit of Disappointment
Victory Over The Lying Spirit

Order Enquiries: Please call our offices or order
online at www.bishopclimate.me

Bishop Climate Ministries
P.O. Box 67884, London, SE5 9JJ
England, United Kingdom
Tel: +44 7984 115900
Email: partners@bishopclimate.org

Yes Bishop! I believe that those who trust in the Lord will never be disappointed so I sow my seed of £25.30 according to Psalms 25:3.

I have enclosed my special seed of deliverance
£ _____

Here is my Prayer request covering the 7 areas I desire the Lord to manifest His Miracles in my life:

_____

_____

_____

_____

_____

_____

_____

(Continued on Back)

Name:

_____

Address:

_____

_____

_____

Telephone:

_____

Email:

_____

NOTE: You can also sow your special seed SAFELY &
SECURELY online via
www.bishopclimate.org/donate.aspx

Printed in Poland
by Amazon Fulfillment
Poland Sp. z o.o., Wrocław

54367356R00026